Ajax

For example

W. C. Tuttle

Alpha Editions

This edition published in 2024

ISBN : 9789366382210

Design and Setting By
Alpha Editions
www.alphaedis.com
Email - info@alphaedis.com

As per information held with us this book is in Public Domain.
This book is a reproduction of an important historical work. Alpha Editions uses the best technology to reproduce historical work in the same manner it was first published to preserve its original nature. Any marks or number seen are left intentionally to preserve its true form.

Contents

AJAX, FOR EXAMPLE..- 1 -

AJAX, FOR EXAMPLE

BY W. C. TUTTLE

"Horse sense," says "Magpie" Simpkins, "consists of knowing something that no school-teacher could pound into your head with a pile-driver. It's a sort of an initiative and referendum that books can't tell you about, and if you ain't got it, Ike, you might as well get you a loaf of bread, a jug of wine and hide out in the brush, where you won't hamper folks with your idiocy. There was Ajax, for example."

Magpie hooks his spurs into the top of the table and leans back in his chair. He knows there ain't no argument, but hopes I'll find one. I agrees with Magpie—for once. I'll tell you why I agree with him, and maybe you'll agree with me.

Me and you both know that there's educated fools. If I can have my choice I'll take the fool that never got educated in preference to one what absorbed everything he found in books, 'cause the educated one can't even crawl into a blanket without peering into a book to see the definition of the word "crawl," the proper uses of a blanket, and the procedure according to precedent.

Yessir, there was Ajax, for example.

Me and Magpie are cooking breakfast in our cabin on Plenty Stone Creek one Summer morning, when we hears footsteps approaching on horseback. Magpie steps to the door with a pan of bacon in his hand and peers outside. He takes one look and tries to scratch his head with the pan, the same of which leaves our hog-meat on the floor.

Then he looks back at me.

"Ike, come here! It's either a mistake or I'm mistaken."

I walks over and takes a look. Looks like one of Sam Holt's rat-tailed broncs, but the rider—whooee! I don't blame Magpie for dropping the bacon. I'd 'a' dropped a stick of dynamite if I'd had one.

I'll begin at the top and work on down. First we have a hat. She looks like a cross between a ordinary hard hat and a campaign lid, being as she's sort of flat on the top. Under said hat cometh hair, which seems to grow straight out.

Then we have a pair of funeral-rimmed specs forking the longest, skinniest nose I ever seen. I feels that it must blow about the same note as the stopped-down E string on a fiddle. The chin of the critter seems to be so long that the weight of it holds his mouth open.

We have with us now the neck. To speak like a poet I'd say that he had the neck of a swan. Maybe not so graceful, but longer. His shoulders shows a heap of neglect, and from there he just sort of slopes off to his feet, which is some slope, if you asks me.

Riding with his elbows has made his sleeves pull up almost to his shoulders, and hanging on with his knees has pulled up the legs of his pants until he's setting on most of 'em. He ain't anything for a drinking man to look at—if he likes the taste of liquor.

Me and Magpie stands there sort of weak-like and watches him search his pockets. He ain't said a word yet. The more pockets he searches the less he seems to find. He grunts and reaches for his hip pocket, the same of which seems to bend his legs backwards until his heels catch in that bronc's flanks.

Zowie!

That rat-tailed bronc resents such familiarity, with the result that said apparition lands setting down in our front yard while the insulted bronc wends its way home.

I plumb forgot to mention that this person carried a little valise on the saddle-horn. Yes, it came off with him.

He sets there on the chip-pile blinking like a old owl, and then he produces an envelope from his hip pocket. Then he adjusts his specs and peers up at us.

"I beg your pardon," says he.

"You have it," says Magpie.

"You won't catch that bronc this side of Piperock," says I. "He's still throwing sand."

"Ah! Oh, the—er—equine? Ah! Unavoidable, I assure you."

"Setting as you were," admits Magpie. "Good scheme to always watch a bronc's ears, old-timer."

"Pleasant pastime, I have no doubt," he agrees. "Oh, quite interesting. May I ask if either of you gentlemen is Mr. Simpson?"

"Little high and to the right," says Magpie. "I'm Simpkins."

"Ah, yes! Delighted, I assure you. My mistake."

He peers at the letter.

"Very good indeed. Simpkins it is. I beg your pardon."

"You're going to get splinters in you if you don't get up," states Magpie.

"Thank you very, very much," says he, handing the letter to Magpie.

"This is my—er—introductions, Mr. Simpson."

"S-i-m-p-k-i-n-s," spells Magpie.

"Ah, yes. Very simple."

"Yes," says I. "Very."

Magpie opens the letter, and I reads it over his shoulder.

> My Dear Simpkins:
>
> The bearer, Professor Ajax Ulysses Green, B.A., F.H.S., K.P., I.O.O.F., B.P.O.E., etc., etc., is desirous of testing out some pet theory, and I am taking the liberty of sending him to you, knowing that you and Ike will see that he gets what is coming to him. Do with him as you will—and I know you will.
>
> Professor Pettingill joins me in sending you our best regards and hopes some day to see you again. Remember us to Dirty Shirt Jones, and all the rest of the Pelicans we met in the county of Yellow Rock.
>
> Very sincerely yours,
> F. H. Middleton.

> P. S.—As Dirty Shirt says, "For ———'s sake, did you ever see the like?" He really is considered a brilliant man, and devoted to his work. Do as you see fit—but spare him, as Pettingill and myself will not rest well until he returns to Boston and tells of his experiences.

"Professor Middleton is one of my dear, dear friends," explains this alphabetical person sweet-like. "He was primarily responsible for my coming. You may thank him."

"My!" gasps Magpie. "I may, may I? Well, well! Come in, Ajax."

"I prefer to be known as Professor Green, if it is not too much trouble," says he stiff-like, but Magpie grins and says:

"I'm Magpie; this is Ike. You're Ajax. *Sabe?*"

"Rather—er—personal, don't you think?"

"How'd you like Ulysses?" I asks.

"No. If I have no choice in the matter I'd prefer Ajax."

"If I had my choice of weapons I'd take a pickax," grins Magpie. "Are you the hombre what discovered lightning?"

"Oh, no! The original Ajax defied the lightning, don't you know."

"He made a sucker play," says I. "Maybe he didn't *sabe* electricity."

Ajax refused to smoke a cigaret, so we gave him an old pipe that "Polecat" Perkins left in our shack, but he didn't seem to care for it.

"Now," says Magpie, "we'd admire to hear what you came here for."

Ajax crosses his legs, adjusts his glasses and clears his throat. It's some job to clear a throat like his. The best way, I reckon, would be to drop in a can of nitroglycerin like they do in oil-wells.

"I am here," says he, rubbing his hands together, "to study the effects of astragalas splendens on the genus Ovius."

Me and Magpie looks at each other and then at Ajax.

"It is very interesting, don't you think?" asks Ajax.

Magpie walks over to the stove and begins to cut more bacon. After he gets it on the stove he turns to Ajax.

"What do you drink for breakfast?"

"Rarely anything, I thank you."

"You ought to take something," says I.

"Well, if I should, I prefer a beverage of *thea sinensis*."

"My ——!" grunts Magpie. "We're all out of that. Ike, I told you to get us some the last time you was in Piperock."

"It is not necessary at all," says Ajax.

"I know it ain't," agrees Magpie, "but I'd sure like to know what in —— it is."

Ajax drank water. Later on me and Magpie got his dictionary and looked up everything that human beings drink, and we found that that danged word-strangler wanted tea.

He don't *sabe* Blackfeet, Flathead or Chinook, and won't talk United States. We can't understand his wau-wau; so we can see that eventually some of us are going to be badly misunderstood.

If it hadn't been for Professor Middleton we'd have lured Ajax to a tall place in the trail and shoved him off. He wasn't even funny.

If you poked a gun under his nose he wouldn't have horse sense enough to hold up his hands. No, I'll be danged if he would! He'd likely smell into the muzzle, look it over careful-like and then classify it in a language that nobody in Yaller Rock County could interpret.

After breakfast he says—

"I will rest today if you don't mind."

"Rest in peace," says Magpie. "Take root if you must, but for the love of Moses try and bend your back and be sociable. You don't smoke, and if you did swear in your own little way nobody'd understand you. Do you drink?"

"*Spiritus frumenti?*"

"Go to ——! Next time I says good morning to you, Ajax, it will be in sign language. I'm through talking to you, that's a cinch."

"I will not consider it obligatory," says he lofty-like, and I just grabs Magpie's hand in time.

"Don't hold the hand of progress, Ike," says Magpie. "Can you figure out one good reason why I shouldn't kill him?"

"Except that we don't know exactly where to ship his remains. He's from Boston, Magpie, but it ain't like saying, 'He's from Piperock.' You've got to figure that Boston covers considerable space, and until we finds out his home address we better let him suffer. *Sabe?*"

"Where is your home, Ajax?" asks Magpie.

"Home? The habitual abode of one's family?"

I lets loose of Magpie's hand and reached for my own gun, but the coming of Dirty Shirt Jones saves me from killing a fool-hen out of season. Dirty slides off his bronc and nods to us. Then he sees Ajax. He peers at Ajax for a minute and then gets right back on his bronc.

"Get off and rest your feet, Dirty," says I, but Dirty only stares at Ajax and shakes his head.

Dirty shakes his head like a bee was buzzing around his ear. He shuts his eyes, shakes his head hard, and looks again.

"My!" says he awed-like. "I've seen a lot of things in my life. I've seen a tarantaler waltzing with a angle-worm, I have. I've seen a little green devil riding a Gila monster in a race against a horned toad which was ridden by me, but I've always been able to shake 'em loose for a minute. This'n I can't!"

"I am Professor Ajax Ulysses Green," says Ajax stiff-like. "It is extremely embarrassing when one's friends forget the—I—er—it places me in a position wherein I am forced to introduce myself to one whom my acquaintances greet as one of their own kind. Embarrassing, I assure you."

"Ex-cuse me," says Magpie. "Ajax, let me make you used to Dirty Shirt. Dirty, this here is Ajax."

"Name's familiar," says Dirty, scratching his head. "Oh, yes! 'Boiled Egg' Benson had a jassack by that name. I wondered who he named it after and why he used to kick it in the ribs all the time. Poor mule!"

"Maybe Dirty Shirt could help you, Ajax. He's seen about all there is in this country."

"Possibly," agrees Ajax. "I'd be grateful to a startling degree."

And then he turns to Dirty.

"I am out here, sir, to study the effects of astragalas splendens on the genus Ovius."

Dirty spits out his cigaret and clamps his jaws hard.

"Before you do anything, Dirty, appeal to your better nature," says I.

"What do you think, Dirty?" asks Magpie.

"Think?"

Dirty swings his bronc around and talks to us over his shoulder.

"I think you three has had all the fun you're going to out of me. I don't know what it means, but you can all go to —— as far as I'm concerned."

We watches him ride off down the road.

"Is he—er—entirely sane?" asks Ajax, watching Dirty disappear.

"Not now," says Magpie. "A human being can only stand so much. He got bit by a hipwiggler the other night."

"Ah! Quite interesting."

And he writes something in his little book.

Ajax wanted to rest that day, so we didn't bother him none. It gave us a chance to control our natural impulses to kill him, and also gave us a chance to do a little placer work.

I asks Magpie that night if we're supposed to give up our bunk to Ajax, but Magpie gives me one look which is plenty of answers. Anyway Ajax didn't desire it.

"Professor Middleton told me of the wonders of sleeping under the glorious firmament," says Ajax, "and I desire to experience it as he described."

"Fairly well ventilated," says Magpie. "Nice enough unless she rains or a hipwiggler comes along."

"Who is 'she,' and what is a hipwiggler, if I may ask?"

"She?"

Magpie smooths his mustache and scowls at the ground.

"Oh, yes; the hipwiggler. The hipwiggler is a animal. If one comes along and finds you sleeping on the ground it just plumb ruins you for future use. You're dead—that's about all."

"Your—er—friend you spoke about," says Ajax. "Was he sleeping on——"

"Uh-huh. A log saved his life. It's thisaway, Ajax: A hipwiggler is a queer animal. It always prospects a man from his head down to his toes. It gets to the end of you and then starts eating its way back. *Sabe?*

"Dirty Shirt went to sleep with his feet on a log. The hipwiggler comes along, walks to where it strikes the ground and then starts eating. It ain't got no *sabe*—not a bit. This one didn't *sabe* that Dirty had his feet on a log; so it went to the end of the log and starts eating. Logs ain't noways digestible, so it got disgusted and left Dirty alone."

Ajax took it all in and then gets inquisitive.

"Could I procure a specimen?"

"Nope. They only sleep between twelve and one o'clock, and nobody knows where they hole up. To catch one any other time you've got to take a sack in your hands, stand on the stump of a persimmon-tree and make a noise like a loofmad."

"Oh, I see. Quite complicated. More of this later, as I am interested."

"You deserve to be," says I. "If it wasn't for Middleton——"

"Ah, yes. I am deeply indebted to Middleton, the dear fellow. I shall mention him in my monograph."

"Do it," urges Magpie. "I'll do the same—in my prayers."

"I—I feel that I am going to make some wonderful discoveries out here."

"Well," says Magpie, "that remains to be seen, as the feller said when he dug into the Injun's grave."

Ajax gets a little skittish about sleeping outdoors, so he rolls up in a blanket on the floor. Me and Magpie are heavy sleepers, but he woke us up in the night. We sets up in bed and listens to him. He's making a lot of noise like he was trying to move the cabin.

Magpie is just getting up to see what the trouble is when Ajax comes in, grunting and wheezing. Comes a big bump on the floor, a deep sigh from Ajax, and then everything is still again; so we goes to sleep.

In the morning Magpie kicks me in the ribs, and I sets up in bed. There is Ajax laying on the floor with his bare legs bent up over a section of pine log about thirty inches in diameter. Magpie snorts right out, and Ajax sets up.

He looks all around the cabin and then reaches for his pants.

"I thank you for the information, my dear Mr. Simpson," says he. "I feel that the section of the genus Pinus was the means of saving my life. Several times after securing it I felt the deadly hipwiggler travel my entire length, only to fall off the log in surprize. It was a sensation I can not wish for again, but one I feel fortunate to have experienced. I thank you for your timely advice."

Magpie smoothed his mustache and stared at me and we both danged near choked. Ajax sure offered himself as a highway for pack-rats that night.

Then cometh Judge Steele. He's the educatedest hombre in the county. If there's anything he don't know he won't admit it. He owns half-interest in a claim up the creek, and is on his way up there with a pack-load of grub for his pardner.

We asks him in to breakfast 'cause you never can tell when you'll need the friendship of a judge.

"Good morning," says he to me and Magpie, and then he sees Ajax.

"Good gosh!"

"Howdy, judge," says Magpie. "Set in on the bacon."

"Ah!" says Ajax. "A judge. Are you an LL.B.?"

"Nope. Missourian and a stanch Republican."

"Ah! It is refreshing to meet an educated man in the wilds. Where did you matriculate, may I ask?"

"Where did I what?"

"Matriculate."

"I'm on my way to my mine, and I started from Piperock, if it's anybody's danged business."

And then he turns to Magpie.

"Friend of yours?"

"Liability, judge. He's trailing something that ain't here nor never was."

"Huh! What's he after?"

"You tell him, Ajax. Something about strangling the———"

"It is not a subject to cause levity," chides Ajax. "Is there any reason why I should not come here to study the effects of astragalas splendens on the genus Ovius?"

The judge stands up to drink his coffee and then goes out to his horses.

"What do you think, judge?" I asks.

He picks up the lead rope of his pack-horse and ponders the question.

"Ike, I hate to give out a judicial reply as I might be called upon to render a decision from the bench, but I'll say this much: Any jury in Yaller Rock County would convict him without leaving their seats."

He gets on his horse and pilgrims off up the trail.

"How quaint," grins Ajax. "Is he really a presiding judge or did he simply acquire the title as many Westerners are reputed to have?"

"I believe he is," says Magpie. "Danged if I don't believe he is."

"Is what?" asks Ajax.

"Right."

"Ah, no doubt," agrees Ajax foolish-like, and we let the matter rest.

Ajax puttered around for a while and then came to us.

"May I—er—have a piece of rope? Three yards will be sufficient."

"Plenty," agrees Magpie pleased-like.

"You know how to tie the proper kind of a knot?"

"I— Perhaps not, but——"

"The pleasure is all mine," says Magpie.

Ajax looks the knot over interested-like.

"Beg pardon, but will you tell me why you wound the rope around so many times?"

"Thirteen times," says Magpie. "Any sheriff knows how. Now, do you want us to elevate the wagon-tongue or do you prefer a limb?"

Ajax's mouth hangs open for a full minute, and then he seems to catch the point.

"He, he, he! You—you thought perhaps I wanted to make a—er— a swing, I believe they call them. You were spoofing me, I fear. No, I thank you."

And he wandered away across the hills alone.

"Ike," says Magpie; "were you spoofing? A swing! My ——!"

We worked for a while but can't seem to get Ajax out of our minds.

The blamed fool might get lost or bit by a snake. Sidewinders don't respect education. After a while Magpie says:

"Ike, if it wasn't for Middleton I'd let the blamed fool sink or swim, survive or perish, but I'd hate to rob Middleton of a chance to hear Ajax tell his experiences. Reckon we better pesticate around a little and see where he went. I'd admire to find out what he's after."

"He said it was the effects of—" I began, but Magpie looked at me with his sweet smile and I shut up.

Ajax pointed almost due south, but we figured he'd bear a little to the west, so we cut across. We're pilgriming down into a draw at the head of a little fork of Medicine Creek when all to once we busts into a clearing, and Magpie stops.

I bumped into him, and then looked over his shoulder. There is "Doleful" Doolittle, who herds sheep when he's sober enough, and standing in front of him is Ajax.

Them hombres sure show signs of rough usage. Ajax's hat is smashed down over his nose, and he's looking out from between the crown and the brim. His coat is split up the back, and his long legs wabble a heap.

Doleful has lost one sleeve and his belt, the same of which causes him to hang on to his pants, so they won't come down and trip him. If Doleful had twice as much sense he'd be almost half-witted.

"Hear me?" yelps Doleful, shaking his one free hand at Ajax. "I'm tellin' you hereby that I'm aimin' to show you, feller!"

"Very ungrammatical, to say the least," pants Ajax. "Now I wish you to desist. Fisticuffs are a relic of——"

"I *sabe*," says Doleful, spitting on his hands. "Set yourself, feller, 'cause I'm coming wide open like a wolf!"

Boof!

Doleful takes a skip and a jump and lands on Ajax's bosom, and they both went into the alkali. It was some fight. They're both yelling for help in about ten seconds, and then they gets to their feet.

"You long-faced son-of-a-sea-cook, you bited me!" howls Doleful, rubbing his ear.

"It was—uh—but fighting the dud-devil with fuf-fire," wheezes Ajax. "You masticated my e-ear, friend."

"Friend?" yells Doleful. "Don't you call me friend! I hate —— out of you, by ginger! Hold fast, 'cause I'm coming to visit you again!"

Ajax sidestepped this time, and when Doleful stumbled over his legs Ajax fell on top of him. Man, they sure investigated each other. Doleful kicked, whooped and yelped and managed to squirm loose, minus one boot, which Ajax has annexed.

For a minute Ajax seems to show human intelligence by hammering Doleful over the head with the boot. Doleful wails loud and clear and hops away a few feet, where he takes off the other boot and comes back at Ajax.

"God didn't make men equal but boots did," says Magpie, and then them two are at it again.

It was some duel if you asks me, and before they're at it a minute me and Magpie are weeping on each other's bosom. They never seen us. In fact they hadn't been at it a minute until they couldn't see each other.

Pretty soon Doleful makes a wild swing, and the heel of that boot hit Ajax at the butt of his ear. That was plenty for Ajax, who sprawls on his face in the dirt, but Doleful didn't know it. He kept right on, hopping back and forth, whaling away with that boot at something that ain't there.

"Look at the danged fool!" gasps Magpie. "He can't see!"

Just then Doleful makes an extra hard swing, his foot slipped, and the toe of that boot hit him under the chin. He straightens up, shrugs his shoulders like a Frenchman and then falls flat on his back—knocked out, or rather kicked out.

"Honest to ——— that never happened," sobs Magpie. "Aw, it couldn't! He hit himself in the— Haw, haw, haw!"

I haw-haws with him, and we cries a duet.

Pretty soon Doleful gets to his feet, walks around in a circle and appears to be listening. Then Ajax coughs and sets up.

"I've had a gosh-darn plenty," states Doleful in a whisper. "Hear me?"

"I'm sorry," says Ajax.

"You danged hog!" wails Doleful. "I know when I've had a plenty. Where is my boots?"

Ajax feels of his ear like he half-expected to find the boot in there, but when he don't find it he shakes his head.

"I don't know, I'm sure."

"I'm going," states Doleful. "My gosh, it's dark today! I can just see enough to miss hittin' trees, and that's about all. Where are you?"

"T fear I'm not able to give you concise information on the subject," says Ajax painful-like, "because I am not aware of my exact position.

- 13 -

If it will enlighten you to any extent I will say this much; I am on the ground."

"Then you stay there," advises Doleful. "If I step on you don't get sore, 'cause I don't mean nothing but good-by. *Sabe?*"

Doleful stumbles across Ajax's feet and goes weaving off through the mesquite, hanging on to his pants and picking up cactus in his feet. Then Ajax gets to his feet and peers around. His specs are still hanging around his neck, and he tries to put 'em on. He's been booted across the bridge of his nose, the same of which makes his specs feel like his nose was in a vise.

He yanks 'em off, and then begins to search his pockets. After a while he finds what he's looking for. Then he feels his way over to a rock, where he gets interested in looking at something—or trying to. We sneaked over and took a look. He's got a compass on the rock, and is talking to himself.

"Unless I am greatly mistaken I traveled due south. Due north would take me—uh— Now would it? Which way did I pursue the Ovius? Well, no matter, as I can not see the compass, therefore I am lost. Perhaps my shadow will inform me of the position of the sun, and by taking the time of day——"

He turns and peers at the ground.

"Futile," he mutters. "There is no shadow. No matter, as my watch is not running. Still I am lost. Not knowing the proper procedure in such a case, I will endeavor to remain stationary until such a time as I may regain the use of my optic nerves. I will think of a remedy."

"Raw beefsteak is hyiu stuff," suggests Magpie. "Ever try it?"

Ajax almost hopped out of his shoes. He peers at us, and then:

"Ah! Raw steak? I greatly prefer mine medium, *en casserole*."

"It's no use, Ike," sighs Magpie. "I had hopes that he'd been hit so hard that he'd talk our language, but I'm a poor guesser. You take one side, Ike, and I'll take the other."

Ajax led like a old pack-horse and didn't have much to say. We asked him why he was sore at Doleful, and he said the idea was absurd.

We tied some raw meat over his eyes, and by supper-time he was able to feel the difference between a knife and a fork.

"Maybe some day you *hombres* will stay in the East where you belong," says Magpie disgusted-like. "You sure gallop in where natives fear to sneak."

"We scientists must suffer that the masses be informed," explains Ajax.

"You ain't going to get a lot of publicity by fighting a boot duel with a half-witted herder," says I.

"It was no violence of my making, I assure you, Mr. Harper. I was chasing the elusive Ovius when this vulgar person came between us. He used very insulting adjectives—very! My lips could never repeat the strange things he said. Naturally I resented. I descended to the level of a brute, and fought as my ancestors fought."

"I've heard of boot-leggers," says Magpie, "but you must 'a' sprung from a family of boot-fighters, Ajax. Did you hit him first?"

"I did not. Nor second or third. In fact he pummeled me for some time before I seemed to grasp his intentions, and then I retaliated."

"You ought to carry a boot," advises Magpie. "Feller like you ought to go heeled all the time. What do you aim to do next?"

"Next?"

Ajax rubs his sore eyes and looks up at Magpie.

"I shall certainly persevere until I have observed fully the effects of astragalas splendens upon the——"

But me and Magpie went out and left him talking to himself.

We helped Ajax bring in his foot-rest that night and watched him go to bed with his feet thirty inches higher than his head. He's so all-in that he never felt the pack-rats that night, and the next morning he's a sorry-looking hunk of scientific humanity.

His clothes are about seven-eighths to the sere and yaller leaf. His valise don't contain nothing but a book, some papers and a box of pills. Magpie looks him over from all angles.

"Somebody will kill you, Ajax, if you dress thataway," says Magpie. "In memory of Professor Middleton me and Ike will have to dress you civilized-like, I reckon."

We got him into an old pair of boots, one of my shirts and an old sombrero of Magpie's. He looks like ———, but he don't know it. Then he wants another length of rope.

"You going back to the same place?" I asks.

He considers it a moment, and shakes his head.

"I don't believe I will. That vulgar person might accost me again, and I have no time to waste in combat. I will try in another direction, if it makes no particular difference."

"Me and Ike are neutral," says Magpie.

"If you'd tell us just about what in ——— you're hunting for, maybe we'd advise you."

"Oh, thank you. You see I wish to observe the effects of astragala———"

"You're welcome!" yelps Magpie. "Go ahead, and may you die in your boots."

"I fear that is impossible," says Ajax. "The boots belong to you."

"Happy birthday!" yelps Magpie. "They're yours, Ajax. Go to it."

"I will do my best, sir," says he, and we watches him going over the hills, dragging his rope behind him.

"Just plain crazy, Ike," declares Magpie. "Plain crazy."

"Not Ajax," says I. "Nossir! That feller is plumb fancy crazy. He's gilt-edged, perfumed and embroidered, Magpie. He knows a million dollars' worth of things that won't never do him any good—things that other fellers like him have found out; and now he's out here to find out something to pass on to them. It won't never do him nor anybody else any good—but they'll be glad."

We knocked off work late in the afternoon. I laid down on the bunk while Magpie fixes a kettle of beans. He's standing in the door of the cabin, pouring the water off them beans, when all to once there comes a hunk of lead, knocks the kettle out of Magpie's hand, and hives up in the foot of our bunk. Then comes the crack of a rifle.

I sees Magpie elevate his hands, and I slips loose my six-shooter. Then here comes "Mighty" Jones, covering Magpie with a rifle.

Mighty owns the only herd of goats in the county, and each and every one of them shaggy things is nitroglycerin on legs. I figures that Mighty has gone crazy from herding same, so when he turns sideways to me I slams a .45 slug into the loading-plate of his rifle.

That slug seems to cause consternation, being as it explodes some of Mighty's magazine, and when a magazine full of 45-70s begin to heave and surge, it's no place for a timid person.

Magpie turns a flip-flop into the cabin, and Mighty tries to dig himself into our chip-pile. I pilgrims out there and looks at Mighty.

"Why for the hands-up stuff, Mighty?" I asks. "You peeved?"

"You dang well know I am! You know why, too—blast you! I only seen one of you, but you two are pardners, and—I'll see you in jail. I'm going to get the sheriff, me!"

"Plain crazy, Ike," says Magpie sad-like. "Plain crazy."

"Very plain," I agrees.

"I'll see you both in jail—betcher life!" wails Mighty. "Sure will."

"Better see a eye doctor, Mighty," advises Magpie. "You're seeing things."

"You'll see something—dang you both!"

And Mighty fogs off down the trail.

"Poor old coot," says Magpie. "Can't help feeling sorry for him, Ike."

"Uh-huh. He was a good old buggy but he's done broke down."

"No question about the buggy part, Ike."

We fixed up our pot of beans and wondered where Ajax is. We ate supper and wondered some more about Ajax.

Then cometh Lindhardt Cadwallader Sims, knowed as "Scenery." We always figured that Scenery was sheriff by default, being as two of Magpie's friends forgot to vote, and Scenery won by one vote. He's about knee-high to a he-human, and has darned near polished all the epitaph off his star in six months. He squeaks when he walks and squeaks when he talks, which makes him a pathetic person among his feller men.

The danged little imitation has a six-gun in his hand when he shows up in our doorway. He peers at us mean-like and clears his throat. I'm just about to pour some beans into my plate, but I takes one look at his gun and swings back with that kettle and let her fly. It was a good shot. She just turns over once and hit him right in the chin.

He staggers backward, drops his gun and begins to claw at them beans. Sudden-like he remembers his gun and goes pawing around for it. I swings the door about half-shut when I hears a biff and a grunt, and Scenery Sims comes into that door on his hands and knees. He hops to his feet fighting mad, and squeaks like a bull fiddle:

"You assassinators is all under arrest! Hear me? You can't monkey with no officer of the peace thataway and get away with it. Magpie, you daw-gonned, long-whiskered———"

Magpie stopped his yelps by picking him up and throwing him out of the door. Scenery was just sailing out as Ajax starts to come in, and they met. When an irresistible jackass meets an immovable educated fool there is something going on.

Them two misfits of the human race went into a clinch and hugged each other like long-lost brothers. They got up fighting blind, went into another clinch and rolled under Scenery's bronc.

For a few seconds there ain't nothing but hoofs, boots and dust to be seen. Then it gets too warm for a buzzard-headed bronc, and said animal leaves its master to fate and an educated fool.

Ajax was a lot stronger than he looked. He squirmed loose, grabs the sheriff by the neck and the seat of the pants and cast him far away.

Poor Scenery! He rolls over a few times and staggers to his feet. He whales away with both fists at nothing, crosses his feet and falls down again.

Then he gets up and starts off down the road. He walks a few steps and then runs a few. Then he does it all over again, like he was expecting a kick in the rear every time he steps.

Ajax has set down on the ground and is trying to dig the alkali out of his mouth and eyes. He sure is a sight. Me and Magpie walks over to him, and Magpie says—

"Say, professor, we'd admire to know if it was you who knocked Scenery into our cabin."

"Scenery?"

He peers up at us and then blinks shut again.

"The general aspect, as regards variety or beauty, or the reverse, of a landscape?"

"My ——!" says I. "He asked you in a lady-like manner: Who knocked Scenery into our cabin? The man you fought. *Sabe?*"

"The—the man I fought?" stutters Ajax. "Did I—I fight a man?"

"Say," says Magpie, "did you get hit so hard that you don't *sabe* things? What did you think you was mopping the earth with?"

"I—er—really——" Ajax mops some more dirt out of his features and peers around— "I—er—suppose I must take your unsupported word for it, but I—I thought at the time that I was being attacked by a specimen of the genus Ovius."

Magpie kicks the empty bean-kettle into the cabin, and me and him follers it inside. Pretty soon Ajax looks in. He peers all around and then begins to search outside.

Me and Magpie went out there and looked around, too. Then Ajax starts circling the cabin, and me and Magpie follered him like a pair of bird-dog pups follering an old dog, but we don't find anything. Pretty soon Ajax sighs deep-like.

"Well, it isn't here, it seems."

"Maybe you lost it some other place," suggests Magpie.

"No. I had it when I arrived."

"——!" grunts Magpie. "What was it, Ajax?"

"The—er—specimen of the genus Ovius."

I grabs Magpie just in time. Ajax never did know how close he skidded to the graveyard that time. Magpie was so mad that he wouldn't come into the cabin while I throws a feed into Ajax.

"There should be a drastic legislation against the careless use of firearms," states Ajax. "Would you believe it—" he pokes a fork at me like he was trying to see if I was done—"some careless person, evidently shooting at random, nearly struck me? I was a little south of here, returning with my specimen, when I detected a singing noise past my ear. Immediately following came the report of a firearm.

"In endeavoring to ascertain the location of the miscreant I became entangled with my specimen, and luckily we fell into a depression behind an outcropping of granite formation. Luckily the depression was filled with a thick growth of mimosaceous shrub, which screened us from view.

"I feel sure that the target was located upon or near that granite outcropping, because in a few minutes I could hear the marksman carrying on a conversation like this, omitting the vulgarity, of course:

"'Pshaw! Missed entirely!'

"And then he seemed heartily ashamed of himself, as he said:

"'Too bad! I should have had higher aspirations.'

"The last may not be correct, but at any rate he mentioned something about holding higher, which amounts to the same."

"Yes," says I; "he was careless, Ajax. I feel sorry for him."

"Perhaps I should have extended my sympathy," says Ajax. "But—er—really I was in no position to think of the niceties of social custom."

"What was you doing all this time?" asks Magpie from the doorway.

"I—er—I was trying to preserve my hold upon the Ovius."

I seen Magpie walk out about fifty feet, throw his hat on the ground and hop up and down on it. This Ovius is getting under his hide.

"I will persevere," says Ajax determined-like. "I must persevere."

"All right, Percy," says I. "Don't let us stop you."

Me and Magpie talked things over, but we can't figure it out.

"That's the —— of it, Ike," says Magpie. "If Ajax was a human being he could tell us what he's after, but education has plumb ruined him for conversation. I reckon we've got to give him plenty of rope, and he'll hang up some place."

"He's used up enough rope to hang all the rustlers in Montana," says I. "He had one specimen, Magpie, but somebody shot at him——"

"Rotten shooting!" snorts Magpie. "There is such things as mob law, and if he don't give us a chance to see what he's after I'm going to turn myself into a mob and make him talk something we can *sabe*.

"What in —— is a Ovius? As far as I can remember there ain't never been one seen here. None of the old-timers has ever spoke of any such a thing, Ike. There ain't nothing in the Injun language that sounds like it."

"Well," says I, "what is astragalas splendens?"

"There you are!"

Magpie waves his arms and walks in a circle.

"There you are, Ike. Both of us holds a blank hand, so we just splits the pot. I reckon I'll likely kill Ajax tomorrow."

"And never find out what he's after?"

"There are things better left unknown, Ike. Let's go to bed before we mention something that we can't explain."

Ajax is writing in his little book by the light of a candle, and when we come in he stops.

"Pardon me," says he to Magpie. "Has anything ever been written regarding the hipwiggler?"

"Nun-not that I knows about. It ain't what you'd call popular."

He thinks it over for a while, and then he sort of says to himself:

"It could be named after me. What an honor!"

"Yes'm," admits Magpie. "You can be a father to it if you want to."

"If I could only secure a specimen!" he wails. "I must! I will!"

He hops off his seat and walks up and down the cabin.

"You spoke of something about securing one by making a noise like a—a——"

"Loofmad?" asks Magpie.

"Exactly. A loofmad. Is it a—er—difficult sound to make?"

"Nope. Easy for lots of folks."

"Would you mind giving me a demonstration?"

"Not me. I did once, and I almost got killed."

"Ah! Is it dangerous?"

"It is and it ain't. You'd be safe, Ajax."

"Will you teach me?"

Ajax stops in front of Magpie and holds out his hands like Magpie had something to give him.

"Teach you? Man, you're born to it. No, I can't tell you how to do it, but the proper note is in your voice every little while, only you don't know it."

"Is it a gift?" asks Ajax.

"Merry Christmas!" explodes Magpie. "If it is I hope nobody knows when my birthday is, and that Sandy Claws goes blind."

"Interesting but vague," says Ajax, and goes back to his book.

Yes, Ajax slept with his feet in the air again.

Me and Magpie talks over the events of the day, but we can't figure it out. We can't figure why Mighty wishes to hold us up, and why he sends Scenery up there with blood in his eye. We asks Ajax the next morning if he's done anything wrong, but he shakes his head.

"I never have done anything wrong," says he.

"This is a great little country to establish a precedent," says Magpie. "A herder of goats comes here yesterday and shoots a bean-pot out of my hands. Later on the sheriff comes up—but you know that. Do you know why they comes here?"

"I haven't an idea."

"I know you ain't, but I thought maybe you had a hunch."

Ajax got himself a rope this time. He hunted around until he found an old sack, and then he sets down to look in his little book.

"Today," says he, "I am going to make a supreme effort to secure valuable data, and I wish to ask a few questions. Is the hipwiggler a vegetarian or of the carnivora, and what is its habitat?"

"The hipwiggler," says Magpie, "eats anything and is fond of children. It is of the hootchie-kootchie family. Hootchie, meaning hip, and kootchie, meaning to wiggle. The great difference between it and anything else is in its shape, size, actions, color and odor."

"Hootchie-kootchie?" asks Ajax. "Is that—er—an Indian word?"

"Uh-huh. The Camelpunchers."

"Has the hipwiggler a distinctive odor?"

"You dang well know it has. You look for something that you never seen nor smelled before. *Sabe?* Catch it and bring it here, and if it ain't a hipwiggler we'll tell you."

"I see. We will have an elimination proceedings."

"Somebody will be, that's a cinch," grins Magpie.

Ajax tightens the rope around his waist, picks up his sack and faces the east.

"I gird up my loins and fare forth. Today I will complete my quest. I bid you good morning, gentlemen."

We watches the blamed fool pilgrim across the hills.

"You've got to admire him for sticking," says I, but Magpie snorts:

"Yeah? Might as well give three cheers for a cactus, Ike."

"Doughgod" Smith comes past about dinner-time and stops to smoke a cigaret.

"Seen a posse today," grins Doughgod. "Some bunch. Scenery Sims, Mighty Jones and Doleful Doolittle. Put them three on a two-by-four island and they couldn't find each other."

"Where did you see 'em, Doughgod?" asks Magpie.

"They left town about an hour before I started. Pointed towards Mighty's place."

Doughgod rode on, and me and Magpie ponders things. That's some posse to go after anybody. Pretty soon Magpie sniffs the air. I sniff a little too, and then we hear Scenery Sims' squeaky voice.

"Halt! You darn fool—halt!"

We steps around the corner of the cabin and sees a queer sight. In the middle of the trail stands Ajax. Standing between his long legs is a goat—a sick-looking goat.

Ajax has got the sack over his shoulder, and when he sees us he swings it to the ground.

Above him on the hill is Scenery with a rifle in his hands, and about sixty feet behind Ajax is Mighty, hanging on to his nose. Below Ajax, standing on the side of the hill with a rock in each hand, is Doleful.

"Stand still, dog-gone you!" squeaks Scenery. "You're under arrest!"

"It is all very peculiar," says Ajax sick-like. "I don't know what it all means, and I———"

Ajax picks up his sack and starts for us.

"Stop him, Magpie!" yelps Scenery. "Shoot the darn fool!"

Ajax stops and looks foolish.

"Will somebody explain things?" asks Magpie, holding his nose.

"He's a thief," says Scenery. "Caught with the goods, too. He stole thet goat from Mighty Jones."

"Well," says I, "why don't you arrest him, Scenery? He ain't heeled."

"Not me! I don't want him."

"I demand his arrest!" yelps Mighty.

"Shut up, Mighty!" squeaks Scenery. "He's been arrested five minutes; ain't you, feller?"

"You mentioned such a proceeding," admits Ajax.

"The law is satisfied."

"What you got in the sack, Ajax?" I yells.

"I am not sure, but I think it is a hipwiggler."

"He tried to steal my sheep," stated Doleful. "He assaulted me and——"

"Hipwiggler ——!" snorts Mighty. "He's got a polecat in that sack. Him and that goat are inoculated against any smell from now on and forever. Amen."

Ajax stands there and looks foolish. He can't smell nothing. There is such a thing as getting too much. The goat swallers hard and leans against Ajax. I feel sorry for the goat.

"Well," says Magpie. "you might as well take your goat, Mighty."

"Not me!" yells Mighty. "I'm off that goat forever."

"Well, it's sort of a deadlock," says I. "Ajax is arrested in name only and the owner of the stolen property refuses to take it back."

Just then Judge Steele rides in from the mine. We explains things to him, and he looks wise.

"Clean case against him, judge," states Scenery. "He's got the goods on him."

"Think I can't smell?" snorts the judge. "This is an open-air case."

He pounds on his saddle-horn.

"Hear ye, hear ye, hear ye! This honorable court is doing business. The prisoner will stay where he is. Are you guilty or not guilty?"

"I have no idea," says Ajax weary-like.

"Prisoner, does that goat belong to Mighty Jones?"

"I have no idea."

"Call it and see if it comes to you, Mighty," suggests Magpie.

"Like ——!"

"Let the goat loose and see who it goes to," suggests the judge.

"Whoa!" yelps Mighty. "Don't do that! I don't know how he ever got the rope on it, but I do know it's the champion butter of the world. You stick with it, feller, and get time off for good behavior."

"This is the same one I had yesterday," states Ajax. "It—er—struck the sheriff, I believe."

"Haw! haw! haw!" whoops Magpie. "It upset our sheriff something awful."

We considers things for a while, and then the judge says:

"According to my own reckoning there ain't nothing to be done, but I has to pass an opinion. Being as the prisoner, smelling as he does, is of no value to the prosecution, and the plaintiff refuses to take back his alleged property, I adjudicates thusly:

"The prisoner will be banished on his own recognizance. Feller, you better go away off some place. *Sabe?* Take your clothes and burn 'em and jump in the river or vicy versy. Given under my hand and seal this fifth day of August in the year of our Lord, and the County of Yaller Rock.

"Now I'd admire why a freak like that does things like he's done?"

"I was desirous of observing the effects of astragalas splendens on the genus Ovius."

"The —— you was!" snorts the judge. "Find out?"

"No. I was almost prepared for the experiment when this unforeseen contingency arose."

"My ——!" grunts Magpie. "He was sure going to do something awful."

"It is nothing to——"

Ajax dropped his rope and stooped to pick it up; and didn't finish his sentence, 'cause that goat hit him dead center and Ajax and his sack turned a cartwheel. The polecat came out of the sack and tangled with the goat, and then both of them started back down the trail towards Mighty.

Mighty must 'a' got his property back, 'cause as far as we can see 'em Mighty is still in the lead, but it's almost a cinch the goat will win out in the end.

Ajax watches 'em for a minute and then starts for the cabin.

"Wait!" snaps Magpie. "I'll get your belongings for you."

"I am going away," says Ajax sad-like; "going where intellect is appreciated. I came here on a scientific mission, and I find that research work is not appreciated."

"We may not be strong for you, Ajax, but it's a cinch you're too strong for us," says Magpie, tossing the valise to Ajax.

"Good-by, Ajax," says I. "Tell Middleton hello for us."

"I shall tell him something for myself," says he, picking up his valise. "Most surely I shall speak to Middleton about you both."

We watches him pilgrim down the trail, exuding odors of which there is no imitation.

"Magpie," says the judge, "have you any idea what he wanted?"

"Not in my language, judge. I'm going to write to Professor Middleton and ask him what it is. I reckon Ajax came to the wrong place."

"Let me know, Magpie," squeaks Scenery. "I'd admire to hear what it was."

We didn't hear no more about Ajax, and about three weeks later we're down at Piperock and got a letter from Middleton. We got Scenery, and the three of us went up to Judge Steele's office.

Magpie opens the letter and reads it aloud to us:

> Dear Magpie and Ike:
>
> Professor Green returned. Tell me about the thing he calls a hipwiggler. He dropped some information to Pettingill regarding it, but refuses even to nod to me. In fact he is very reticent over the whole matter.
>
> He started to tell Pettingill about the "loofmad." Pettingill wrote it out and happened to spell it backward. Now Green won't speak to Pettingill. Please tell us why a vigilance committee in Silver Bend made him burn his clothes, which by the way contained his money. We are very anxious to hear all about it.

> You ask the meaning of Green's statement—to study the effects of astragalas splendens on the genus Ovius.

Magpie's lips move slow-like over it, and then he hands the letter to us. The three of us bends over it and reads where he left off:

> He meant that he wished to study the effects of loco-weed on sheep.

The four of us leans back against the wall and look at each other.

"Magpie," says the judge, clearing his throat and brushing off his vest, "Magpie, what do you think of too much education?"

"On a par with astragalas splendens, judge."

"To which," says the judge, "I will say, '*E pluribus unum.*'"

All of which might be true, but Ajax was our first example.

THE END

www.ingramcontent.com/pod-product-compliance
Ingram Content Group UK Ltd.
Pitfield, Milton Keynes, MK11 3LW, UK
UKHW031339260325
456749UK00002B/295